Melanie Graham • Stanton Procter

English Time 6

Workbook

2nd Edition

OXFORD
UNIVERSITY PRESS

OXFORD
UNIVERSITY PRESS

Great Clarendon Street, Oxford, OX2 6DP, United Kingdom

Oxford University Press is a department of the University of Oxford. It furthers the University's objective of excellence in research, scholarship, and education by publishing worldwide. Oxford is a registered trade mark of Oxford University Press in the UK and in certain other countries

First published in 2011
2017
10 9 8 7 6

ISBN: 978 0 19 400559 3

Printed in China

This book is printed on paper from certified and well-managed sources

ACKNOWLEDGEMENTS

Illustrations by: Lyndall Culbertson, Vilma Ortiz Dillon, Ruth Flanigan, Patrick Girouard, James Hart/Sylvie Poggio Artists Agency, Richard Hoit, Meredith Johnson, Jon Mitchell/Beehive Illustration, Dana Regan, Mick Reid, Jorge Santillan/Beehive Illustration.

Cover illustration by: Paul Gibbs

Original characters developed by: Amy Wummer

Do You Remember?

A. Read and check the best response.

1. Can I help you?
   - ☐ Yes, please. What kinds of pie do you have?
   - ☐ They're ten dollars each.
2. Can you take a message?
   - ☐ I'll give him your message.
   - ☐ Sure. Who's calling?
3. So, how's your family?
   - ☐ She's doing better today.
   - ☐ They're fine.
4. Are your parents home?
   - ☐ No. They went to a movie.
   - ☐ What should I do?

B. Read the question. Write the answer.

1.

Is he giving a speech?

No, he isn't. He's ______________________

____

2.

Is she playing the flute?

____

____

3.

Are they building a sand castle?

____

____

4.

Did he get a good grade?

____

____

C. Read and write.

1. once → __________ → three times → four times
2. January → __________ → March → __________
3. __________ → usually → often → sometimes
4. day → __________ → month → year

D. Read the question. Write the answer.

1.

How did she play the drums? ____________________

____

2.

How much chicken soup did they have? __________

____

3.

How often do you feed the birds? ________________

____

E. Read and match.

1. If I skip lunch, •
2. When I was little, •
3. I chopped vegetables •
4. I had two slices •

- • I could count to ten.
- • by myself.
- • of roast beef.
- • I'll be hungry.

A. Fill in the blanks. Then number the sentences in the correct order.

exchange	cash	last	gift	credit	sale
sweater	Thanks	total	you	doesn't	

______ Is it still on ______________?

______ I'll take this ______________.

______ Charge. Here's my ______________ card.

______ Okay. ______________ for your help!

______ Of course. He can ______________ it or get a refund.

______ Hello. How can I help ______________ today?

______ Yes, it is. Today is the ______________ day.

______ This is a ______________ for my son. If he ______________ like it, can he exchange it?

______ The ______________ is $35.99. Will that be ______________ or charge?

B. Look at A. Read and circle True or False.

1. The gift is for a girl. True False
2. If the woman's son doesn't like it, he can get a refund. True False
3. Today is the last day the sweater is on sale. True False

A. Look and write.

1. 
2. 
3. 
4. 
5. 
6. 
7. 
8. 

B. Look and write.

1. The pajamas are ______ beside the ______
2. ______ in front of ______
3. ______ behind ______
4. ______ near ______

Focus Time

A. Read and check.

1. 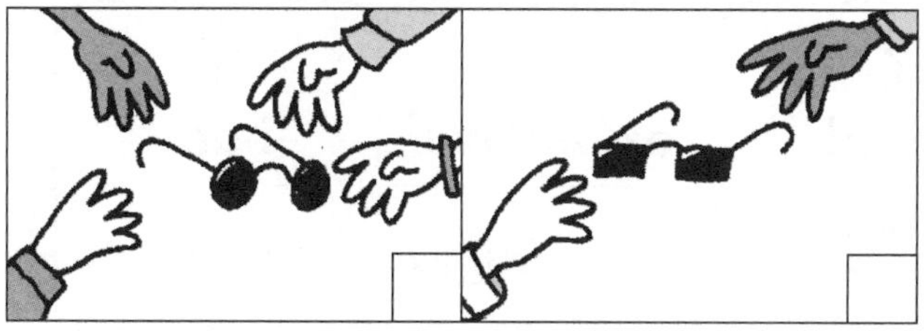

more popular

2. 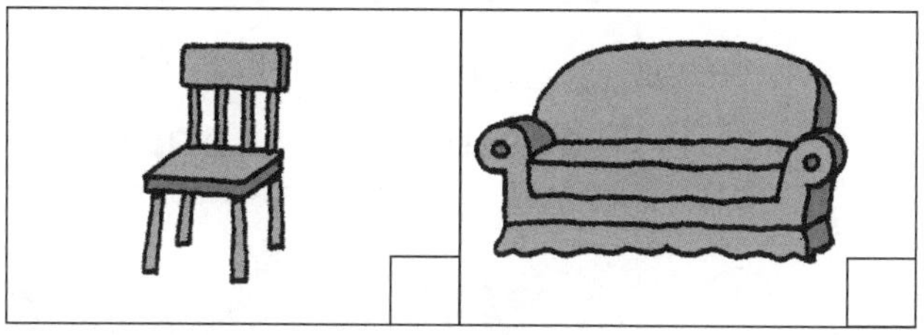

more comfortable

3. 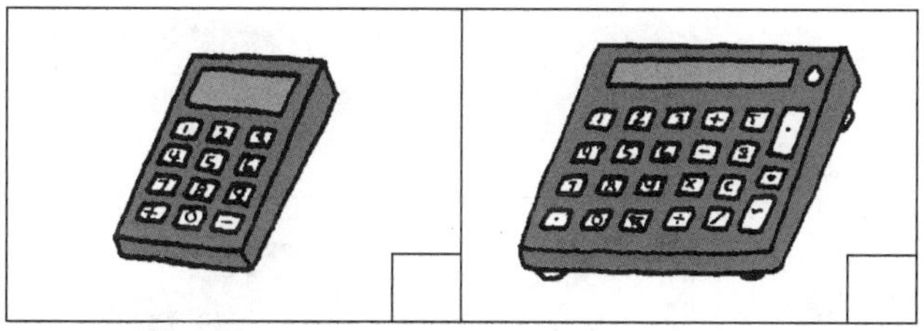

better

4. 

worse

5. 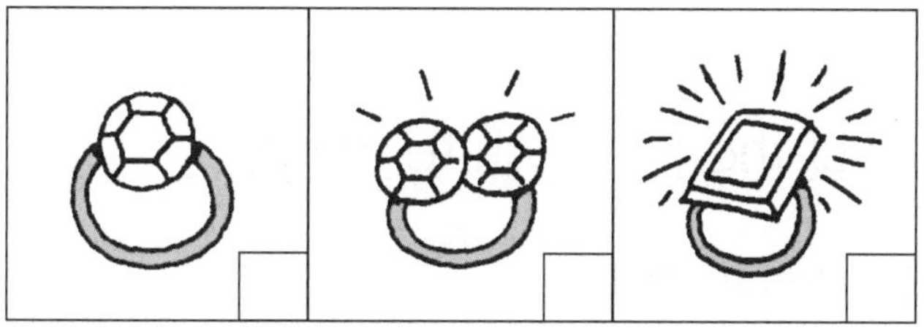

the most beautiful

6. 

the most expensive

7. 

the best

8. 

the worst

B. Read and write.

1. 

The gray pants are more ____________ than the white ones. The black pants are the most ____________

2. 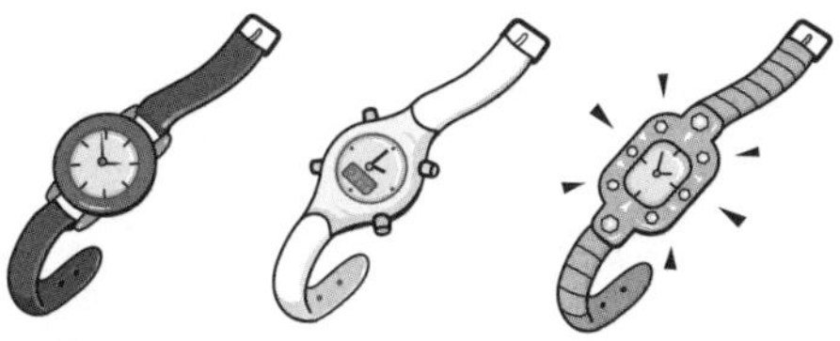

The white watch is better ____________ black one. The gray watch is the ____________

Look and write.

	Ⓐ beautiful	Ⓑ popular	Ⓒ good	Ⓓ expensive	Ⓔ bad
①	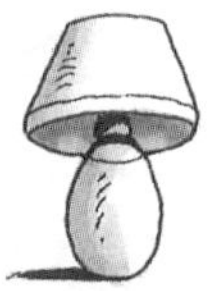		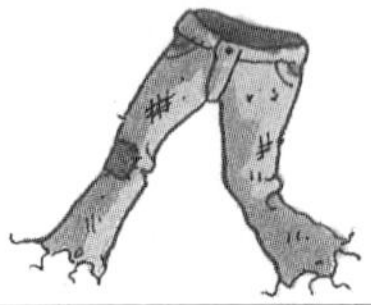		
② more			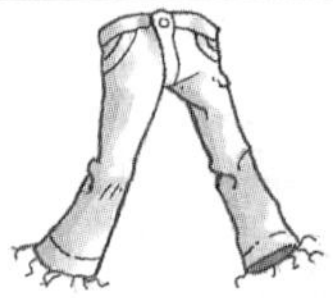		
③ most					

1. A2 A1 The gray lamp is more beautiful than the white lamp.
   A3 The black lamp is the most beautiful.
2. E2 E1 ______
   E3 ______
3. C2 C1 ______
   C3 ______
4. B2 B1 ______
   B3 ______
5. D2 D1 ______
   D3 ______

A. Read.

Dear Gabby,

Dear Gabby,

I have a problem. My best friend, Annie, gave me some sunglasses for my birthday. They were expensive. She bought them at June's Department Store. But they are the ugliest sunglasses in the world! They aren't comfortable either. I don't want to wear them. What should I do? I don't want to hurt Annie's feelings.

Ted

Dear Ted,

Wow! This isn't easy. But I have a suggestion for you. The next time you see Annie, tell her how you feel. Be honest. Maybe she will help you exchange the sunglasses at June's Department Store. Good luck!

Gabby

B. Read and circle True or False.

1. Ted thinks the sunglasses are comfortable. True False
2. Gabby doesn't have a suggestion for Ted. True False
3. Ted doesn't want to hurt Annie's feelings. True False
4. Gabby says, "Be honest." True False

C. Read the question. Write the answer.

1. What is Gabby's suggestion for Ted?

____

2. What is Ted's problem?

____

A. Read and circle True or False.

1. A couch is more comfortable than a chair. True False
2. Brown is more popular than blue. True False
3. Popcorn is better than ice cream. True False
4. Parrots are more beautiful than eagles. True False
5. Cats are better than dogs. True False
6. Soccer is better than basketball. True False

B. What do you think? Look at the picture and write three sentences.

1. ______________________________
2. ______________________________
3. ______________________________

C. Read and write the answers.

______________________________ ______________________________

Conversation Time

A. Fill in the blanks.

Alaska	cruise	dream	vacation	Ted	usually	sounds		
wish	skiing	too	him	never	family	hear	go	Hi

B. Look at A. Read the question. Write the answer.

1. Where is Ted? ____
2. What is Emily's dream vacation? ______________________________
3. What is Annie's dream vacation? ______________________________

A. Unscramble and write.

1. 

etuc

____

2. 

usby

____

3. 

eitqu

____

4. 

ldo

____

B. Read the question. Write the answer.

1. 

Is she weak?

No, she isn't. She's ______________________

2. 

Is he stubborn?

____

3. 

Is he thirsty?

____

4. 

Is the cake light?

____

Match and write.

1. 

2. 

3. 

4. 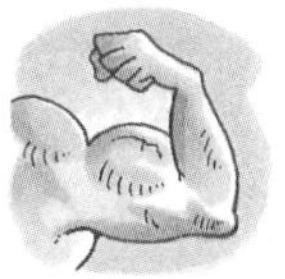

5. 

6. 

7. 

8. 

9. 

10. 

a.  ______________________

b.  light as a feather

c.  ______________________

d.  ______________________

e.  ______________________

f.  ______________________

g.  ______________________

h.  ______________________

i.  ______________________

j. 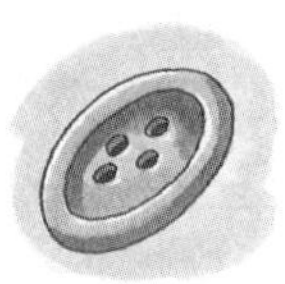 ______________________

A. **Read and circle True or False.**

1. 

The police officer isn't as strong as the firefighter. The firefighter is as strong as an ox.

True False

2. 

The girl isn't as old the grandmother. The grandmother is as old as the hills.

True False

B. **Look and write.**

1. Emily isn't as strong ________________________
   Annie is as ________________________
2. Dave ________________________
3. Dan ________________________
4. Tom ________________________

Reading Time

A. Unscramble and fill in the blanks.

oclo	aspregenss	brnsuun	ciseru
ibg	kelorsnnig	oolsp	culonibrsa

From: Annie@Sunnyville.com
To: Emily@Sunnyville.com
Date: October 8
Subject: Ted's vacation

Hi, Emily!

Ted wrote to me. He's still on vacation. He says the cruise ship is really ______________. He's so lucky. My dream vacation is a ______________.

Ted says there are 2,000 ______________ on the ship. The ship is as ______________ as a town, and there are five ______________. There is even a computer room.

Ted says he has a ______________. He saw a shark through his ______________, too. Isn't that scary?

They're going to go ______________ in the Bahamas today. Wow! He'll be home tomorrow.

Your friend,
Annie

B. Read the question. Write the answer.

1. How many passengers are on the cruise ship?

____

2. Where is Ted going to go snorkeling?

____

3. When will Ted be home?

____

Your Time

A. Read and write.

1. If you are 100 years old, you're as ______
2. If you work 16 hours a day, you're as ______
3. If you can eat ten slices of beef, you're as ______
4. If you get a good grade, you're as ______

B. Read and write.

1. I'm as happy as a clam when I ______
2. I was as busy as a bee when I ______
3. I'm as quiet as a mouse when I ______
4. I'm as hungry as a bear when I ______
5. I was as cute as a button when I ______

C. Write about your dream vacation. Then draw.

My dream vacation is ______

3 Conversation Time

A. Circle the mistakes and write.

1.  Hey, Annie! Look to my ribbon! My pie one first prize at the state fair!

____

2.  congratulations.

____

3.  Thank. Is there anything wrong? You don't look berry happy.

____

4.  Yeah. I don't full very happy.

____

5.  Why? What happens?

____

6.  My tie came in last place. It tested awful.

____

7.  Check up. You can try again last time.

____

8.  No, it hasn't matter. I give up.

____

9  Don't give down! I'll help you. We can walk together after state.

____

B. Look at A. Read and circle.

1. Whose pie came in last place?

a.  b. 

2. Whose pie won first prize at the state fair?

a.  b. 

3. Who doesn't feel very happy?

a.  b. 

4. Who says "You can try again next time"?

a.  b. 

A. Look and write.

1.  She's proud. ______

2.  ______

3.  ______

4.  ______

B. Read and write.

1.  She has a math test tomorrow. She didn't study. She's ______

2.  His dog ate his shoe. He's ______

3.  She won first prize. She's ______

4.  He got a bad grade. He feels ______

5.  She fell off her bike. She feels ______

6.  Her brother won first prize. She's ______

7.  He ate seven burgers. He's ______

A. Read and match.

1. Isn't he envious?
2. Aren't they angry?
3. Weren't you full?
4. Wasn't he worried?

No, they aren't. Yes, he was. Yes, we were. Yes, he is.

B. Look and write.

Yesterday

Now

1. Wasn't he worried? ________________
2. Isn't he worried? ________________
3. Wasn't she surprised? ________________
4. Isn't she surprised? ________________

C. Write the questions and the answers.

1.

Dear Dad,
I saw a snake yesterday!
Annie

________________ scared?

Yes, ________________

2.

Dear Mom,
I ate six burgers!
Ted

________________ Ted full?

________________ is.

A. Read and write.

B. Write the questions and the answers.

1.  ________________ worried? ________________________

2.  ________________ embarrassed? ________________________

3.  ________________ surprised? ________________________

A. Choose the correct word and write.

SUNNYVILLE *Weekly*

SEPTEMBER 5

THE STATE FAIR CONTESTS

The ________ (recipe / competition) was fierce at this year's state fair in Sunnyville. There were 20 different ________ (contests / fairs). Carl and Casey Martin won the ________ (three-legged / winner) race. John Hamilton's dog, Beef Bone, won the dog contest. We ________ (entered / talked) with John Hamilton after the awards ________ (ceremony / contest).

Sunnyville Weekly: ________ (Hate / Tell) us about your dog. What ________ (name / kind) of dog is he?

John Hamilton: He's an interesting dog. He's big, and he likes to eat pizza!

SW: Wow! Are you going to ________ (enter / invent) the dog contest at the next fair?

JH: Yes, of course. But I am going to enter with a ________ (recipe / new) dog.

SW: Good luck, Mr. Hamilton.

JH: ________ (Thank / Hate) you very much.

B. Read the question. Write the answer.

1. What does Beef Bone like to eat? ________________
2. Who won the three-legged contest? ________________
3. Will John Hamilton enter the dog contest next year? ________________
4. How many different contests were there this year? ________________

A. Read and write the answers.

1. Aren't you full when you eat a lot of pizza? ____________________
2. Aren't you scared when you see a spider? ____________________
3. Aren't you uncomfortable when you sit in a small chair? ____________________
4. Aren't you embarrassed when you forget your homework? ____________________
5. Aren't you proud when you get a good grade? ____________________
6. Aren't you surprised when you win a contest? ____________________

B. Read and write the answers.

1. When do you feel angry?

____

2. When do you feel proud?

____

3. When do you feel scared?

____

4. When do you feel full?

____

5. When do you feel envious?

____

C. Read and write the answer.

____

____

____

Cross-curricular 1

A. Choose the correct word and write. Then write the letter.

a. This reaction is 'fight or flight'. He can run away. Or he can stay and ______________. (flight / fight)

b. He's safe now. ______________ (Fear / Blood) can be good!

c. He breathes quickly so his body gets more ______________. (fear / oxygen)

d. The man is fishing. Look, there's a bear!

e. He's scared. His ______________ (brain / heart) beats faster. Blood goes to his muscles.

f. He runs home quickly. His body's reaction helps ______________ (hurt / protect) him.

B. Answer the questions.

BIOLOGY Q & A

1. What's the body's reaction to fear called?
A: ______________________________
2. What does 'flight' mean?
A: ______________________________
3. What happens to the heart when we're scared?
A: ______________________________
4. How does the body get more oxygen?
A: ______________________________
5. How does more oxygen help the body?
A: ______________________________
6. Is fear good for us?
A: ______________________________

ask-dr.bio.com

Conversation Time

A. Read and match.

1. Hi! What are you doing? •
2. Do you know what you're doing? •
3. All right. The first ingredient is flour. One cup of flour. •
4. Stir in two teaspoons of baking powder and one quarter teaspoon of salt. Then, mix in three quarters of a cup of milk and two egg whites. •
5. I said three quarters of a cup of milk and two egg whites, not two cups of milk! •

• Oh, no. What a mess!

• Got it. What's next?

• Of course. There's a recipe in that cookbook. Read it to me, okay?

• Got it. Two teaspoons of baking powder and one quarter cup of salt. Then, two cups of milk and three to four egg whites!

• I'm making pancakes. Do you want to give me a hand?

B. Look at A. Read and circle.

Pancakes  **C = cup**  **t = teaspoons** 

egg whites	1	2	5
baking powder	2 t	1 t	1/4 t
salt	3/4 C	1 t	1/4 t
milk	1/4 C	3/4 C	1 C
flour	1 C	2 t	1/4 C

Unscramble and write. Then number the pictures.

1. tes teh bleta

   ____

2. laenc het tasble

   ____

3. defe hte erosh

   ____

4. ribng hte ifrst iad tki

   ____

5. upt no usnscneer

   ____

6. apnit het gnsi

   ____

7. xif hte encfe

   ____

8. bidlu a eifr

   ____

9. kmae stiucsib

   ____

10. lapy wtih het dgo

   ____

A. Read and write.

	Every day, I...	Now, I'm...	Yesterday, I...
1.	set the table	setting the table	____________
2.	make biscuits	____________	____________
3.	____________	building a fire	____________
4.	____________	____________	played with the dog
5.	feed the horse	____________	____________
6.	____________	fixing the sign	____________

B. Look and write.

1. Every day, they ____________
2. Now, ____________
3. Yesterday, ____________

C. Read and write.

1. They're ____________, aren't they?
   Yes, they are.
2. He ____________, didn't he?
   Yes, he did.

A. Read the question. Write the answer.

1. 

Annie is fixing the fence, isn't she?

____

2. 

She's making biscuits, isn't she?

____

3. 

He set the table, didn't he?

____

4. 

He fed the horse, didn't he?

____

B. Read and write.

1. ______________________________

didn't he?

Yes, ______________________________

2. ____________ played ____________ dog,

____________ they?

No, ____________ They ____________

3. ______________________________

____________ isn't she?

____________ is.

4. ____________ cleaning ____________

isn't he?

____________ he ____________

A. Read.

White Water Ranch

Do you like swimming and rafting? The White Water Ranch is the best place for a rafting vacation!

Located in the Rocky Mountains, the White Water Ranch is beautiful. At our 100 acre ranch, we have something for everyone. We have mountain trails for hiking and two rivers for swimming and rafting. If you like horses, you can round up cattle with our cowboys. Bring your saddle!

You'll like the fresh air at our ranch. You'll feel great! Call 1(800) 555-5411 for more information today!

B. Read the question. Write the answer.

1. What's the best place for a rafting vacation?

   ____

2. Where is the White Water Ranch?

   ____

3. What should you bring?

   ____

4. How will you feel at the White Water Ranch?

   ____

C. Read and write.

1. At our 100 acre ranch, ______________________________
2. You can round ______________________________
3. We have two rivers for ______________________________
4. You'll like the ______________________________

A. Read and circle True or False.

1. I put on sunscreen.	True	False
2. I went horseback riding.	True	False
3. I brought a first aid kit.	True	False
4. I swam in a pool.	True	False
5. I set the table.	True	False
6. I made pancakes.	True	False
7. I played with a dog.	True	False
8. I ate biscuits.	True	False
9. I wrote an e-mail.	True	False

B. Make up a recipe. Pick six ingredients. Write.

butter milk flour sugar water chocolate chips eggs
popcorn pickles strawberries mushrooms cup teaspoon

Recipe

My recipe has ______________________________

____

____

____

____

____

5

Conversation Time

Unscramble and fill in the blanks. Then write.

watch	seen	was	show	change	boring	storms	shows

1. 

______	!	Hey	the	Don't	channel	.

____

2. 

But	.	time	my	it's	favorite	______	for

____

3. 

I	.	watching	*Super Sweepstakes*	______	Well	,

____

4. 

______	.	Let's	Game	watch	comedy	this	are	.	______

____

5. 

.	it	______	not	already	funny	I've	it's	and	,

____

6. 

minute	a	.	Wait	channel	this	Let's	.	______

____

7. 

lightning	A	show	!	about	______	Cool	!	Yeah	.

____

A. Look and write.

1. At 1:00, ______________________
2. At 5:00, ______________________
3. At 9:00, ______________________
4. At 11:00, ______________________

B. Find and circle the words.

d	a	l	w	r	o	u	h	l	h	t	s	u	n	a	m	i	x	e	r	e	p	l
c	r	o	t	y	p	h	o	o	n	r	o	i	i	q	b	l	i	z	z	a	r	d
a	t	o	e	r	f	l	a	r	d	e	a	r	t	h	q	u	a	k	e	c	s	t
q	e	m	u	j	a	l	c	p	a	s	l	a	n	d	s	l	i	d	e	u	f	a
n	y	p	l	g	a	y	o	r	v	m	u	e	d	a	b	j	l	u	q	v	i	b
b	i	u	r	g	h	i	m	o	a	i	t	h	u	n	d	e	r	s	t	o	r	m
p	v	n	c	k	y	t	f	z	d	h	e	e	v	e	b	o	a	r	g	l	e	a

A. Read and number the pictures.

1. scary 2. exciting 3. loud 4. awful 5. windy 6. dangerous

B. Read and circle.

1.

Has he ever seen a tornado? / landslide?

Yes, he has. / have. It was scary. / loud.

2.

Has he ever / never been in a / an blizzard?

No, he hasn't. / haven't.

3.

Has she ever been in a typhoon? / drought?

Yes, she has. It was / were exciting. / windy.

Practice Time

A. Read the question. Write the answer.

1. 

Has he ever been in a drought?

Yes, ______________ It ______________

2. 

Has he ever seen a tsunami?

____

3. 

Have they ever seen a fire?

____

B. Look at the chart. Write the questions and the answers.

	scary	loud	awful	windy	exciting	dangerous
earthquake	Sue	Liz	Al			
landslide		Jim				Al
typhoon	Al		Jim	Sue		Liz
blizzard					Jim	

1. Has Al ever seen an earthquake?

   ______________ It was ______________

2. Has Sue ever been in a blizzard?

   ____

3. Has Jim ______ been ______ typhoon?

   ____

4. ______ Liz ______ seen a blizzard?

   ____

5. ______________ seen ______________

   Yes, he has. It was exciting.

6. ______________ been ______________

   Yes, he has. It was dangerous.

A. **Fill in the blanks with the questions.**

When do blizzards occur? Where should I go if there is a blizzard?
What can a blizzard do? What is a blizzard?

Frequently Asked Questions About Blizzards

Q: ______________________

A: A blizzard is the most dangerous kind of winter storm. It's very cold and windy. Wind speeds can be as fast as 35 miles per hour. There is a lot of snow.

Q: ______________________

A: Blizzards occur in fall and winter. In the United States, most blizzards occur in January, February, and March.

Q: ______________________

A: Blizzards can damage buildings and roads. Blizzards can cause car accidents because people can't see when there is a lot of snow.

Q: ______________________

A: Go inside a building and stay warm.

B. **Read the question. Write the answer.**

1. What can blizzards cause?

____

2. In a blizzard, how fast can wind speeds be?

____

3. What can blizzards damage?

____

A. Read and circle Yes or No.

1. Have you ever seen a tornado? Yes No
2. Have you ever been in a thunderstorm? Yes No
3. Have you ever seen an earthquake? Yes No
4. Have you ever been in a blizzard? Yes No
5. Have you ever seen a fire? Yes No
6. Have you ever been in a typhoon? Yes No
7. Have you ever been in a drought? Yes No

B. Read and write the answers.

1. Have you ever been in a hospital emergency room?

____

2. Have you ever seen a lightning storm?

____

3. Have you ever played soccer after school?

____

4. Have you ever watched a comedy on TV?

____

C. Read and write the answers.

____

____

____

____

____

A. Read and match.

1. Smaller earthquakes after a large earthquake •
2. Tectonic plates are •
3. An earthquake happens if tectonic plates •
4. Scientists measure the size of an earthquake with •
5. An earthquake is always strongest •
6. Scientists compare the size of earthquakes •
7. Earthquakes that are 5 or more on the Richter scale •
8. Sometimes there are tsunamis, landslides, and •

- • move and make the ground move.
- • at the epicenter.
- • with the Richter scale.
- • are called aftershocks.
- • fires after a large earthquake.
- • a seismograph.
- • big, flat rocks.
- • can cause damage to buildings.

B. Read and write. Use the words from Exercise A.

SUNNYVILLE *Daily News*

SUNNYVILLE NEWS – EARTHQUAKE HITS SUNNYVILLE

There was an earthquake at 10:45 A.M. yesterday morning in Sunnyville. Scientists from the Earthquake Center said that the earthquake was more than 5 on the [1] ____________________. Mike Turner, a scientist from the Earthquake Center, said, "There are big, [2] ____________________ rocks under the Earth. We call them [3] ____________________. When the tectonic plates move, the [4] ____________________ can sometimes move. This causes an earthquake. We use the Richter scale to [5] ____________________ the size of earthquakes."

The [6] ____________________ of the earthquake in Sunnyville was 25 miles north of Sunnyville. Scientists measure earthquakes with a [7] ____________________. This also shows where the epicenter of an earthquake is.

There were ten, small [8] ____________________ after the earthquake in Sunnyville. The earthquake caused a little [9] ____________________ to homes and stores. There was also a small fire, but no one was hurt.

A. Read and write. Then match.

1. How _______ I help you today? •
2. _______ Annie? I haven't seen her around lately. •
3. _______ up. You can try _______ next time. •
4. _______ it to me, okay? •
5. Let's watch this _______ •
6. Will that be cash or _______ •

- • All _______ The first _______ is flour.
- • I'll _______ these shoes.
- • She's on _______
- • No, it _______ matter. I _______ up.
- • Charge. Here's my _______ card.
- • Yeah! A _______ about typhoons! Cool!

B. Read the question. Write the answer.

1\.

What's the total?

____

2\.

What is Annie's dream vacation?

____

3\.

Did Joe's pie come in last place?

____

A. Circle the odd word or phrase.

1. typhoon / hungry / blizzard
2. calculator / watch / surprised
3. clean the stable / busy as a bee / cute as a button
4. drought / embarrassed / worried
5. proud / pajamas / scared
6. sunglasses / stuffed animal / put on sunscreen

B. Read the question. Write the answer.

1. 

What's she doing?

____

2. 

What do they see?

____

3. 

Is he envious?

____

A. Read and write.

1. 
I want to eat six slices of pizza, three bags of chips, and some apple pie. I'm as hungry as ______

2. 
My grandmother is 92 years old. Her friends are 96 and 94 years old. They're as ______

3. 
My father works every day. He never goes on vacation. He's as ______

4. 
My mother bought me a little puppy. I love it! It's as ______

B. Read and write.

1. good ⟶ better ⟶ ______
2. popular ⟶ more popular ⟶ ______
3. bad ⟶ ______ ⟶ the worst
4. beautiful ⟶ ______ ⟶ the most beautiful

C. Unscramble and write.

1. | ever | you | a | drought | been | Have | ? | in |

______

2. | aren't | making | They're | biscuits | ? | they | , |

______

3. | she | ? | proud | Wasn't |

______

A. Write the questions and the answers.

1.

______________________, didn't he?

Yes, ______________________

2.

Aren't they angry?

____

3.

She's playing with the dog, isn't she?

____

4.

______________________ been in a flood?

Yes, ______________________

5.

Wasn't ______________________

Yes, ______________________

6.

____

Yes, ______________________ awful.

B. Read and write.

1.

The gray ______________________

expensive __________ white __________

2.

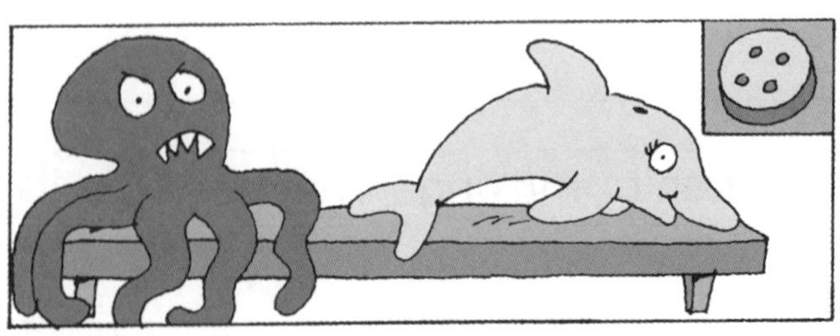

The octopus ______________________

cute ______________________ the dolphin.

A. Read the question. Write the answer.

1. Who gave Ted sunglasses?

____

2. Where did Ted go on vacation?

____

3. Who won the dog contest at the state fair?

____

4. What can you round up at the White Water Ranch?

____

5. When do most blizzards occur in the United States?

____

B. Number the pictures.

1. Dear Gabby
2. Hi, Emily!
3. The State Fair Contests
4. The White Water Ranch
5. Frequently Asked Questions About Blizzards

Review 1: Your Time

A. Read and write the answers.

1. Have you ever won first prize?

____

2. Do you want to go on a cruise?

____

3. Do you have a dog?

____

4. What's your favorite TV show?

____

B. Read and circle True or False.

1. I've been to Alaska. True False
2. I've made pancakes. True False
3. I've watched a show about tornadoes. True False
4. I've bought sunglasses. True False

C. Read and write the answers.

1. Have you ever been as happy as a clam? When?

____

____

2. Have you ever been as busy as a bee? When?

____

____

3. Have you ever been as quiet as a mouse? When?

____

____

6 Conversation Time

Fill in the blanks. Then number the conversation in the correct order.

Where are	You look	one of each	Do you have
but it's too big	find something	do you think	very well
Try it on	Over there	It comes in	have a medium

[ ]

Excuse me. Can I help you ______________?

Yes. I really like this T-shirt, ______________.

[ ]

Well, what ______________ ______________?

It fits ______________.

______________ terrific.

[ ]

I don't think we ______ ______. Here's a small. ______________.

______________ the fitting rooms?

______________.

[ ]

______________ any other colors?

______________ red, blue, and black.

I'll take ______________.

Read and write. Then number the pictures.

1. make the cappuccino
2. ______ the puzzle
3. ______ the cell phone
4. ______ the portrait
5. ______ the jacket
6. ______ the magazine
7. ______ the game
8. ______ the candy bar
9. ______ the coffee
10. ______ lunch

Focus Time

A. Read and write.

	Present	Past	Present Perfect
1.	drink	______	have / has ______
2.	______	read	have / has ______
3.	______	______	have / has drawn
4.	play	______	have / has ______
5.	______	finished	have / has ______
6.	______	______	have / has eaten
7.	buy	______	have / has ______
8.	______	______	have / has made
9.	______	did	have / has ______
10.	______	______	have / has tried

B. Read and write.

1. She has already ______
2. She hasn't ______

3. He has ______
4. He ______ yet.

A. Read and write.

1. ____________________ already played the game.
2. ____________________ the puzzle ____________________

3. ______________________________________ the portrait.
4. ____________________ the coffee ____________________

B. Look and write.

1.  ____
2.  ____
3.  ____
4.  ____

A. Read.

CD Store Damaged by Landslide

by Mary Smith

Monday's earthquake caused a small landslide in Bryson City. Several feet of water and mud filled many houses. The landslide didn't hurt any people or animals, but there was a lot of damage.

The most extensive damage was in Chris Gardner's store, CD World.

"I was talking on the phone when the earthquake started. Then mud and water started to pour in, and I ran. It was scary," said Mr. Gardner.

Luckily, Mr. Gardner's insurance will pay for new CDs. Repairs have already begun at the store.

B. Read and circle True or False.

1. The landslide hurt some people. True False
2. There was a lot of damage. True False
3. Chris Gardner was scared. True False
4. Repairs haven't begun yet. True False

C. Read the question. Write the answer.

1. Whose store was damaged? ______________________________
2. What caused the landslide? ______________________________
3. What was Chris doing when the earthquake started? ______________________________
4. Who will pay for the new CDs? ______________________________

Your Time

A. What have you done today? Read and circle Yes or No.

1. I have already finished lunch. Yes No
2. I have already eaten a candy bar. Yes No
3. I have already drunk water. Yes No
4. I have already studied English. Yes No
5. I have already played a game. Yes No

B. What have you done today? Read and write the answers.

1. Have you brushed your teeth yet?
   ____
2. Have you watched TV yet?
   ____
3. Have you studied math yet?
   ____
4. Have you had recess yet?
   ____
5. Have you eaten dinner yet?
   ____

C. Read and write the answers.

____
____

____
____

A. Number the sentences in the correct order.

_____ That's funny. I thought your grades were good.

_____ Why not?

_____ How was your report card?

_____ How did you do?

_____ Not very well. Mostly C's.

_____ I don't know. I study hard. I guess I get too nervous.

_____ Pretty good. I got five A's. How did you do?

_____ My homework scores are high, but I don't do well on my tests.

B. Look at A. Read the question. Write the answer.

1. How many A's did the boy get?

____

2. Why doesn't the girl do well on tests?

____

3. Are the girl's homework scores high?

____

A. Look and write.

1. 

Ted got a good grade in ____________________

2. 

Peter doesn't like ____________________

3. 

Mark's favorite class is ____________________

B. Read and match.

1. numbers calculator •
2. sing flute trumpet •
3. exercise eat sleep •
4. cities rivers mountains •
5. draw paint color •
6. plants study planets •
7. soccer play exercise •
8. spell ABC write •

• music
• health
• art
• math
• English
• gym
• geography
• science

A. Unscramble, write, and match.

1. rdeob ____________
2. edinrestet ____________
3. fucdeons ____________
4. derit ____________

B. Unscramble and write.

1.

tired	.	I'm	think	.	history	tiring	is	I

____

2.

He	interesting	.	He's	thinks	interested	.	science	is

____

3.

think	.	They	.	math	confused	confusing	They're	is

____

C. Read and write.

1. 

They're ______________________________

They think history is ______________________________

2. 

They're ______________________________

They think math is ______________________________

A. Read and circle.

1.	I'm	tired. tiring.	I think geography is	tired. tiring.
2.	Ted and Annie are	bored. boring.	They think science is	bored. boring.
3.	You're	confused. confusing.	You think art is	confused. confusing.
4.	John is	interested. interesting.	He thinks health is	interested. interesting.

B. Look and write.

1.

She's bored. She thinks ______________________

____

2.

She's ______________________

____

3.

____

____

4.

____

____

A. Read.

STUDENT NEWS

September 20

TIPS ON LEARNING COMPUTER SCIENCE

1. Get to know your computer! Spend time with it.
2. Always ask questions. Don't be afraid to ask your friends or teachers for help.
3. Pay attention to your computer science teachers. You can learn a lot from them.
4. Study and do your homework every day.
5. Read computer books and magazines. You can find a lot of new information. Read as much as you can!
6. Use computers with your friends. Playing and learning together can be fun!
7. Always have a good attitude. If you are interested in computers and you work hard, you'll succeed.

B. Read the question. Write the answer.

1. Why should you pay attention to your computer science teachers?

____

2. Where can you find new information about computers?

____

3. What should you always have if you want to learn computer science?

____

4. Should you be afraid to ask questions?

____

A. Read and write.

What do you think about geography?

1. **geography** I think geography is ______
2. **history** ______
3. **TV** ______
4. **computers** ______
5. **soccer** ______
6. **English** ______
7. **art** ______
8. **museums** ______

B. What do you think? Compare and write.

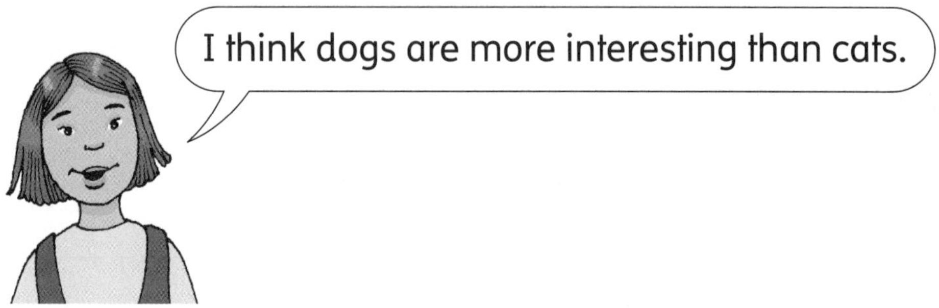

1. soccer / baseball / tiring

______

2. math / science / confusing

______

3. homework / washing dishes / boring

______

8 Conversation Time

A. Circle the correct sentences.

1. Ted, please throw that away.
   Dad, dress throw that way.

2. Why? I'm not finished yet.
   What? I know finished yet.

3. You're not allow to drink by that school.
   You're not allowed to drink by the pool.

4. Ready? Nothing told me.
   Really? Nobody told me.

5. Well, it says so right here. These are the rules.
   Will, is said to write here. This are that rules.

6. No dived. On splashed. No running. I'm sorry.
   No diving. No splashing. No running. I'm sorry.

7. Your should play tennis. Yes don't will to get on trouble.
   You should pay attention. You don't want to get in trouble.

8. What happens if you break the camp rules?
   Why happening is you broke the camp pools?

9. If you break the rules, you can't use the pool for 24 hours.
   In your birds the rulers, You can't use them pull for twenty-four hours.

10. I'll better bet careful.
    I'd better be careful.

B. Read and match.

1. 

2. 

3. 

Ted, please throw that away. Why? I'm not finished yet.

Oh, I'd better be careful. Come on. I'll race you to the other side.

No diving. No splashing. No running. No food or beverages in or around the pool. I'm sorry.

Word Time

A. Look and write.

1. 

He likes to ______________________

He doesn't like to ______________________

2. 

____

____

3. 

____

____

B. What will they do on their next vacation? Look and write.

1.  He'll ______________________

2.  ______________________

3.  ______________________

4.  ______________________

Write the questions and answers.

	write postcards	make crafts	climb mountains
	easy	frustrating	hard
	fun	easy	frustrating
	frustrating	disgusting	exhausting
	easy	hard	easy
	fun	exhausting	fun

1.  What does he ____________________ writing postcards?
____

2.  ____________________ about ____________________ crafts?
____

3.  What ____________________ climbing ____________________?
____

4.  ____________________________________ postcards?
____

5.  ____
____________________________________ frustrating.

A. Read and write.

1. What does she think about ______________________
   She thinks canoeing is frustrating.
2. ______________________
   They think hiking is exhausting.
3. ______________________
   He thinks bird-watching is fun.
4. ______________________
   I think doing jumping jacks is easy.

B. Read. Then answer the questions.

1. What does Alice think about walking on the beach? ______________________
2. What does Peter think about canoeing? ______________________
3. What does Peter think about climbing mountains? ______________________
4. What does Alice think about sharks? ______________________

Reading Time

A. Read and fill in the blanks.

campfire	canoeing	boring	scary	least
tipped over	counselors	camp	making crafts	ride

Dear Annie,

I'm having a great time at ______________ Every day, I ______________ a pony in the mountains. Then we go ______________ We ______________ today, but it wasn't ______________

My ___________ favorite activity is bird-watching. I think it's ___________ I like ___________ I made a kite yesterday. It can really fly!

Tonight we're going to have a big ____________ and the ____________ are going to tell ghost stories. I can't wait!

Your friend,

Ted

B. Read and circle True or False.

1. Ted is having a great time at camp. True False
2. The counselors are going to tell ghost stories. True False
3. Ted goes skiing every day. True False
4. Ted's least favorite activity is making crafts. True False
5. Ted thinks bird-watching is boring. True False

A. Read and write the answers.

1. What do you think about bird-watching?

____

2. What do you think about riding a pony?

____

3. What do you think about catching caterpillars?

____

4. What do you think about making crafts?

____

5. What do you think about climbing mountains?

____

6. What do you think about eating ice cream?

____

B. Make the rules for your own swimming pool.

Swimming Pool Rules

____

____

____

The Swimming Pool is open from ______________ to ______________

C. Read and write the answers.

1. Are you allowed to eat or drink in class? ____________________
2. What happens if you break your parents' rules? ____________________
3. Should you pay attention to your teacher? ____________________

A. Choose the correct word and write.

1. More people speak ______________________ than any other language in the world.
   English / Mandarin Chinese
2. English is the world's ______________________ language.
   international / native
3. People in Australia speak English as their ______________________ language.
   native / international
4. People in England and ______________________ call cookies 'biscuits'.
   Ireland / America
5. Native speakers of English sometimes have different ______________________.
   languages / accents
6. People in ______________________ say they live in apartments.
   Canada / England
7. An accent means the ______________________ of words is different.
   grammar / pronunciation
8. It is important to listen to native ______________________ from around the world so you can understand them all.
   speakers / languages
9. The rules of language are called ______________________.
   grammar / pronunciation

B. Read and write. Use the words from Exercise A.

Sean Kelly, 12
Ireland

Hi, I'm Sean. I'm twelve years old and I'm from [1] ____________. English is my [2] ____________ language. My friend Zac is from New York City and he has an American [3] ____________. I often can't understand his [4] ____________ of English words! Americans sometimes use different words for things. One time, I was in America and I asked Zac's mother for a biscuit. She gave me a kind of bread. I was really surprised! My friend said they call biscuits 'cookies' in America.

Lihua Wang, 11
Canada

Hello. My name's Lihua. I'm eleven. I'm from China but I live in [5] ____________. I'm not a native [6] ____________ of English. My native language is [7] ____________. I think English [8] ____________ is difficult, for example, the present perfect! My parents think it's important to speak good English because it's an [9] ____________ language and people speak English all over the world.

9 Conversation Time

Circle the mistakes and write.

1. What's down, Ted?
   What's up, Ted?
2. I'm waiting four the old exchange teacher. He's going in the Number 15 bus.
3. Are he going to stay win your family?
4. Yes. He's going to sleep for two rest of the year.
5. I can't stand to meat him. Where's his name?
6. It's Paolo. She's from italy. He'll be at school yesterday.
7. Great! Bye the way, did the Number 10 taxi go buy?
8. Yet. It left five hours ago.
9. Oh, yes! I miss the plane. I can believe it.
10. Do worry. The next bus won't be there soon.

A Read and write. Then number the pictures.

1. Mr. Brown is going to work at the bank.
2. Bob likes to ______________________, but he doesn't like fixing the fence.
3. Kim likes to ______________________ on the sidewalk near the park.
4. Ming is an ______________________ She misses her parents.
5. Mr. Jones likes to ______________________, but he doesn't like to play chess.
6. Ms. Farrah likes to cook. She wants to ______________________

B. Read and write.

1.

They like to ______________

____

2.

She likes to ______________

____

3.

They want to ______________

____

A. Read and write for or since.

1. I've studied English ____________________ three years.
2. Bill has played basketball ____________________ he was eight years old.
3. My sister has had a stomachache ____________________ two hours.
4. Emily has painted pictures ____________________ April.

B. Read and write.

1.

2.

3.

4.

1. He's played chess since ____________________
2. His mother worked ____________________
3. ____________________
4. ____________________

C. Look at B. Write the questions.

1. How long has he played chess? ____________________
2. ____________________
3. ____________________
4. ____________________

A. Write the words and phrases in the correct category.

August
four months
Friday
fourteen days
four o'clock
2006
two years
ten hours

for

____
____
____
____

since

____
____
____
____

B. Write the question and the answer.

1.  How long ________________
They've ________________

2.  ________________
____

3.  ________________
____

4.  ________________
____

A. Choose the correct words and fill in the blanks.

Dear Ms. Smith,

I saw your sign at the Sunnyville Supermarket. The Foreign Exchange Program looks very ______ (interesting/boring)! I ______ (would like/like) to visit a foreign country.

I want to ______ (experience/interest) a different ______ (semester/culture). That sounds so exciting. I also want to study French and ______ (make/like) new friends. Can I go to France? Do you have a host ______ (family/country) in France? I would like to ______ (live/adjust) in France for a ______ (day/semester).

My parents and I ______ (could/would) like to find out more about your ______ (program/experience). We'll ______ (send/come) to your office next week.

Sincerely,

Brent Parker

B. Read the answer. Write the question.

1. ______

He wants to live in France.

2. ______

He saw the sign at the Sunnyville Supermarket.

3. ______

He wants to live in France for a semester.

4. ______

He wants to study French and make new friends.

A. **Choose words to complete the questions. Then write answers.**

play chess	have a pet	walk to school	watch TV
play the violin	paint pictures	take the bus	set the table
study English	study math	do laundry	wash the dishes
collect coins	be a student	play games	play soccer

1. How long have you ______________________________

____

2. How long have you ______________________________

____

3. How long have you ______________________________

____

4. How long have you ______________________________

____

5. How long have you ______________________________

____

B. **Read and write.**

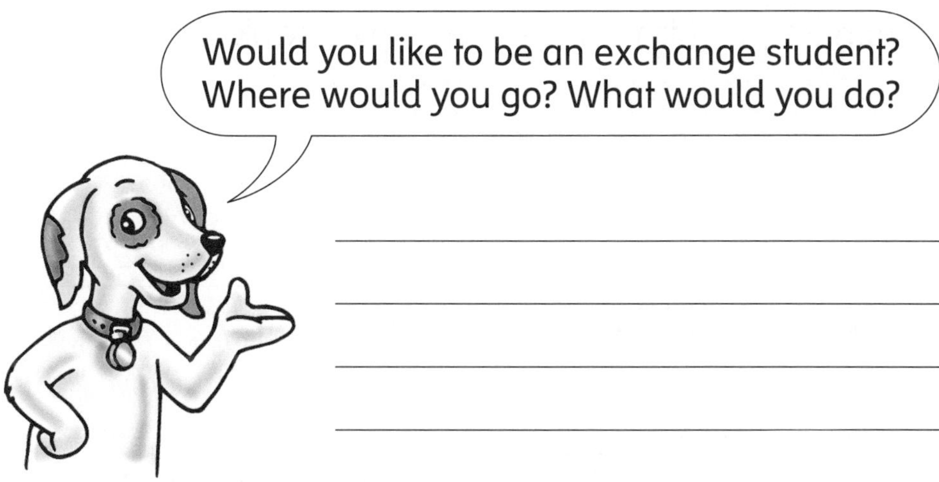

____

____

____

____

____

____

____

Conversation Time

Unscramble and fill in the blanks. Then write.

party | I'll | go | far | blocks | take | directions | bank | Here's

1. you | ? | please | Can | us | give | the | school | to | ________

____

2. ________ | course | It's | . | Of | not | .

____

3. graduation | going | We're | to | the | . | ________

____

4. ! | That's | later | be | . | ________ | great | there

____

5. map | . | ________ | Turn | light | left | at | . | the | a

____

Go | two | . | ________ | straight | for

____

right | ________ | on | Then | a | . | Elm | Street | the | by | bank

____

6. Right | the | by | ? | ________

____

7. ________ | Elm | down | then | , | Yes | for | blocks | four | .

____

A. **Use the code to write the words. Then number the pictures.**

a	b	c	d	e	f	g	h	i	j	k	l	m	n	o	p	q	r	s	t	u	v	w	x	y	z
↓	↓	↓	↓	↓	↓	↓	↓	↓	↓	↓	↓	↓	↓	↓	↓	↓	↓	↓	↓	↓	↓	↓	↓	↓	↓
z	y	x	w	v	u	t	s	r	q	p	o	n	m	l	k	j	i	h	g	f	e	d	c	b	a

1. ____________________
   wizd gsv klhgvih
2. ____________________
   dirgv gsv klvn
3. ____________________
   wvxlizgv gsv illn
4. ____________________
   yold fk gsv yzoollmh
5. ____________________
   hrmt gsv hlmt
6. ____________________
   xloli gsv yzmmvi
7. ____________________
   xllp gsv nvzo
8. ____________________
   gvoo gsv hglirvh
9. ____________________
   nzpv gsv xzpv
10. ____________________
   hrtm gsv xziw

B. **What do they like to do? Look and write.**

She likes to ____________________

He ____________________

Focus Time

A. Read and write.

	Present	Past	Past Passive
1.	color	________	was/were colored
2.	________	wrote	was/were ________
3.	decorate	________	________
4.	________	________	was/were drawn
5.	________	cooked	was/were ________
6.	make	________	________
7.	sing	________	________
8.	________	blew up	was/were ________
9.	________	________	was/were signed
10.	tell	________	________

B. Read and write.

1. 

Ms. Day cooked the meal. =

The meal was cooked by ________

2. 

Dan blew up the balloons. =

____

3. 

Mr. Day wrote the poem. =

____

Practice Time

A. Read and write True or False.

1. Who drew the posters? The posters were drawn by Digger. __________
2. Who signed the card? The card was signed by Ted. __________
3. Who made the cake? The cake was made by Bob. __________

B. Look and write the questions and the answers.

1. Who blew up the balloons? The balloons ____________________
2. ____________________
3. ____________________
4. ____________________
5. ____________________
6. ____________________

A. Read.

HOME | PHOTOS | FAVORITE THINGS | MESSAGE BOARD

SUE MARTINO'S HOME PAGE

WELCOME TO MY HOME PAGE!

Today, I'm going to tell you about my sixth grade graduation party. Last Saturday, our bash was held in the gym. The room was decorated by all the students. The meal was cooked by our parents, and Ms. Jakes baked a delicious cake. I brought homemade cookies. Everyone liked them!

The entertainment was terrific. A long poem was written and recited by Bob Jones. Our school song was sung by the sixth grade chorus. Music was provided by the teachers.

We had a lot of fun. I can't wait to attend junior high school next fall!

B. Read and match.

1. poem
2. school song
3. homemade cookies
4. meal
5. cake

by Bob Jones | by Ms. Jakes | by Sue | by the parents | by the sixth grade chorus

C. Read the question. Write the answer.

1. Who made the cake? ______________________
2. What will Sue do next fall? ______________________
3. What kind of cookies did Sue bring? ______________________
4. What did Bob Jones do? ______________________

A. **Draw an ✗ on the map. Then write the directions from the O to the ✗.**

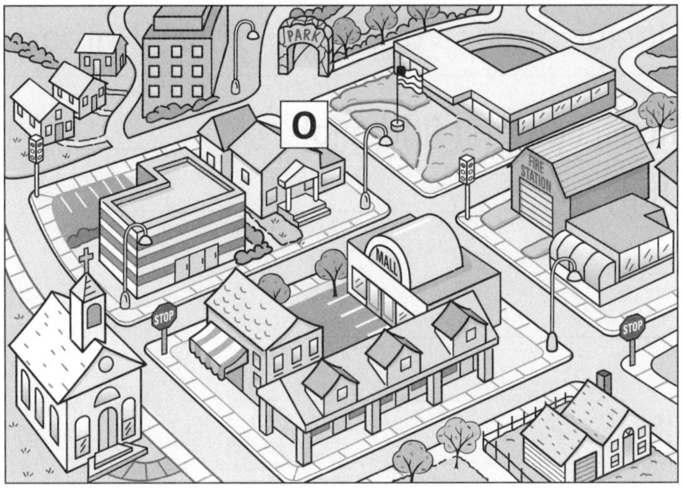

Here's a map. Start at the O.
Go ______

______

______

______

B. **Read and write.**

1. Have you ever written a poem? ______
2. Have you ever drawn posters? ______
3. Have you ever blown up balloons? ______
4. Have you ever cooked a meal? ______
5. Have you ever played chess? ______
6. Have you ever built a fire? ______
7. Have you ever missed a bus? ______
8. Have you ever had a graduation bash? ______

C. **Write about your dinner last night. Use the passive tense.**

______

______

______

______

______

______

A. Circle the incorrect word. Then write the correct word from the box.

visa	weeks	museum	the United States	doctor	poor	ancestor	ship	Harbor

1. The Rossi family was very sick because Mr. Rossi couldn't find a job. ______________
2. Antonio Rossi and his family immigrated to Italy. ______________
3. They went by train. ______________
4. It took two months and it was a difficult trip. ______________
5. They went to Ellis Island in New York Lake. ______________
6. A police officer checked them. ______________
7. Many American citizens have a doctor who immigrated through Ellis Island. ______________
8. The Rossi family didn't need a passport or a citizen then. ______________
9. Today Ellis Island is a popular harbor. ______________

B. Read. Then answer the questions.

Cara McCann immigrated to the United States with her family from Ireland when she was five years old. They went by ship. "I remember it all," said Cara. "The trip was terrible. It was hot and there were so many people on the ship. The trip took ten days." On August 15, 1921, Cara and her family arrived at Ellis Island in New York Harbor. "It was very exciting!" said Cara. "We were on Ellis Island for three hours. Then we entered the United States. All the buildings were so big!" Cara's uncle helped Cara's father get a job. "It was difficult at the beginning. Now I love America and all my family are American citizens."

1. Where did Cara McCann immigrate from? ______________
2. Who did she immigrate with? ______________
3. How did they travel to the United States? ______________
4. How long was the trip? ______________
5. When did they arrive at Ellis Island? ______________
6. Who helped Cara's father? ______________
7. Is Cara happy she immigrated to the United States? ______________

A. Read the question. Write the answer.

1. 

How does the T-shirt fit?

____

2. 

How was her report card?

____

3. 

What are the swimming pool rules?

____

4. 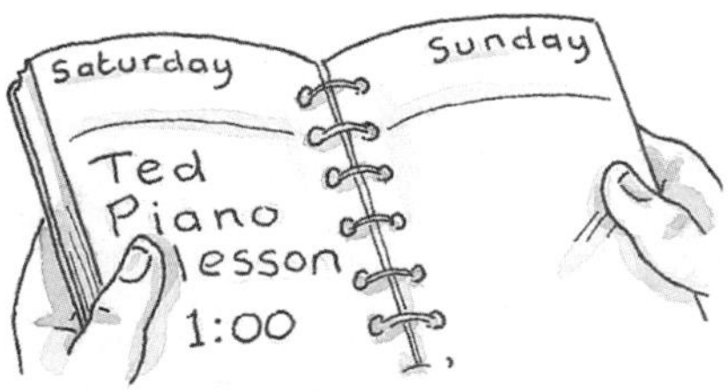

What time is Ted's piano lesson?

____

B. Unscramble and write.

1.

?	help	you	Can	something	I	find

____

2.

throw	.	away	Annie	,	please	that

____

3.

going	to	guitar	I'm	late	lesson	be	for	my	.	downtown

____

4.

by	.	right	Elm	Take	a	Street	bank	on	the

____

A. Read and match.

Sue is climbing the mountain.

Kara is reading the magazine.

Lisa is playing the game.

Jen is riding the pony.

B. What were they doing at 12:00? Look and write.

1. He was making the cappuccino at 12:00.
2. ______________________________
3. ______________________________
4. ______________________________
5. ______________________________
6. ______________________________

A. What do they think? Look and write.

	canoe	hike	fish	climb mountains
easy				
hard				
disgusting				
frustrating				

1.  He thinks ______________________________
2.  ______________________________
3.  ______________________________
4.  ______________________________

B. Read and write **for** or **since**.

1. She's had a cold __________ three days.
2. They've been at home __________ three o'clock.
3. You've worked at the department store __________ June.
4. They've had a pet __________ a year.

A. Look and write. Use already or yet.

1.  He's already ______________________

2.  She hasn't ______________________

3.  ______________________

4.  ______________________

B. Write the questions and the answers.

1. she / a pet? ______________________
   two days ______________________
2. he / sell flowers? ______________________
   six years old ______________________
3. they / play chess? ______________________
   one week ______________________

C. Read and write.

1. Jan wrote the poem. = ______________________
2. ______________________ = The card was signed by Bob.
3. Dan blew up the balloons. = ______________________

Review 2: Reading Time

Read the question. Write the answer.

1. When did the earthquake hit Bryson City?

___

2. Who can help you learn computer science?

___

3. What are the counselors at Ted's camp going to do?

___

4. Why did Brent Parker write to Ms. Smith?

___

5. Where was the sixth grade graduation party held?

___

6. Have repairs begun at CD World yet?

___

7. How can you succeed in computer science?

___

8. What's Ted's least favorite activity at camp?

___

9. What does Brent want to do in France?

___

10. What did Sue Martino bring to the graduation party?

___

11. Where did Ted go canoeing?

___

12. What caused the landslide in Bryson City?

___

A. Read and write ✓.

What do you think about English?

	fun	interesting	boring	easy	confusing
English					
math					
science					
art					
history					
gym					
computer science					
geography					
music					

B. Read and write the answers.

1. What do you think about playing baseball?

____

2. What do you think about catching caterpillars?

____

3. How long have you been a student?

____

4. How long have you lived in your town?

____

5. What's your least favorite class at school?

____

6. What's your favorite class at school?

____

Read and match.

1. What happened?	Nobody told me.
2. Well, what do you think?	Pretty good. I got five A's, two B's, and a C.
3. If he doesn't like it, can he return it?	It fits very well.
4. You're not allowed to eat or drink by the pool at Camp Wildwood.	But it's 4:30. It's time for my favorite show.
5. How was your report card?	My pie came in last place.
6. The first ingredient is flour. One cup of flour.	Of course. It's not far.
7. Give me back the remote.	Yes. It left five minutes ago.
8. Can you please give me directions to the Sunnyville Elementary School?	Of course. He can exchange it or get a refund.
9. Did the Number 10 bus go by?	He's on vacation. His family went on a cruise to the Caribbean.
10. Where's Ted? I haven't seen him around lately.	Got it. What's next?

A. Look and write.

1. 

2. 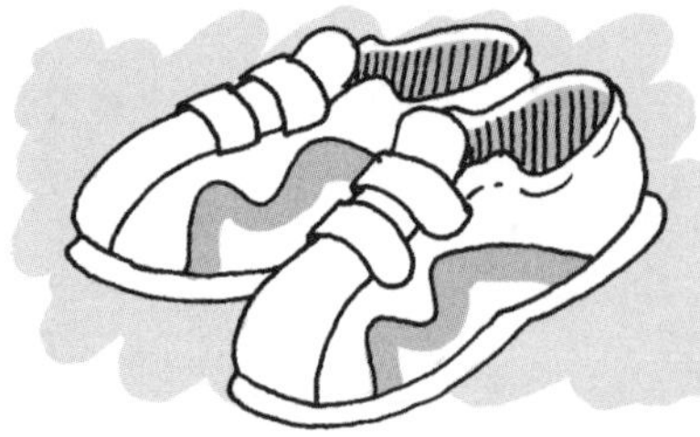

3. 

4. 

5. 

6. 

7. 

8. 

9. 

B. What are they doing? Look and write.

1. 

2. 

3. 

4. 

Focus Time and Practice Time Review

A. Write.

1. he/worried? ______________________

   Yes, ______________________

2. Matt/busy/Bob ______________________

   Bob/a bee ______________________

3. she/catch caterpillars? ______________________

   disgusting ______________________

4. you/teach French? ______________________

   six years ______________________

5. draw the posters? ______________________

   Ivy ______________________

6. He/bored ______________________

   computer science ______________________

7. they/seen/tsnuami? ______________________

   Yes/awful ______________________

B. Read and number the pictures.

1. She has already finished lunch.
2. She hasn't done the puzzle yet.
3. Aren't they discouraged?
   No, they aren't.
4. They're worried, aren't they?
   Yes, they are.

Read and number the pictures.

1. Dear Gabby
2. Hi, Emily!
3. The State Fair Contests
4. White Water Ranch
5. FAQ About Blizzards
6. CD Store Damaged by Landslide
7. Tips on Learning Computer Science
8. Dear Annie
9. Dear Ms. Smith
10. Sue Martino's Home Page

Word List